CU01213134

Original title:
Steaming Cups, Falling Snow

Copyright © 2024 Creative Arts Management OÜ
All rights reserved.

Author: Harris Montgomery
ISBN HARDBACK: 978-9916-94-462-2
ISBN PAPERBACK: 978-9916-94-463-9

Snug Warmth Beneath the Winter Sky

As snowflakes dance on chilly air,
We find our place within the glow.
A crackling fire, a gentle flare,
The world outside draped deep in snow.

Wrapped in blankets, tight and warm,
Hot cocoa steams, a rich delight.
Winter's chill brings a cozy charm,
As we embrace the quiet night.

The window's frost, a frosted lace,
Twinkling stars in the vast expanse.
In this snug corner, we find our space,
Lost in whispers, a soft romance.

Together here, the world is bright,
With laughter ringing through the hall.
Beneath the winter sky's pure white,
In moments shared, we have it all.

Heartfelt Sips in a Shimmering World

In the soft glow of dusk,
Tea leaves swirl like dreams,
Each sip a gentle hug,
Wrapping warmth in seams.

Steam dances in the air,
Whispers of stories old,
Moments caught in porcelain,
Memories yet untold.

A flicker of candlelight,
Shadows brush the walls,
With each heartfelt toast,
Love's invitation calls.

Together in stillness,
Time slows, gently drifts,
Heartfelt sips shared slowly,
In a world that shifts.

Teapot Tales Beneath the Flurries

Inside, the kettle hisses,
Winter winds start to play,
Each pour a tale unwinds,
As snowflakes float and sway.

Beneath layers of white,
We gather, laughter bright,
Teapot tales of wonder,
In the cozy twilight.

The sweet scent of spices,
Fills the room with delight,
Each cup a warm embrace,
In the chill of the night.

Footprints trace the window,
Nocturnal dances call,
To the warmth of the fire,
And the teapot's thrall.

Warmth Cradled in Gentle Hands

Like sunbeams on the skin,
A cup cradled in palms,
Embers glow softly within,
Comfort in tender balms.

Moments weave like fabric,
Threads of laughter and cheer,
In the heart's quiet corner,
Connection crystal clear.

With every sip of warmth,
The world feels less aloof,
Hearts beat in unison,
Under the same roof.

Cups raised in unison,
To the stars above the pines,
We find our quiet refuge,
In the simplest designs.

Serene Sips as Snowflakes Fall

Outside, the snowflakes waltz,
In patterns soft and light,
Inside, serene sips flow,
As day melts into night.

The world is hushed and white,
In this tranquil embrace,
Between heartbeats and breaths,
A moment, pure grace.

Each drop carries whispers,
Of dreams yet to unfold,
As we sit together,
In warmth against the cold.

Serene sips linger long,
In this quiet retreat,
With love wrapped around us,
Life feels whole, complete.

Warmth Swirling in Frosty Air

In the vale where chill winds blow,
Whispers of warmth begin to flow.
Soft blankets hold a cozy light,
Frosty breath meets the fire's bite.

Laughter dances, crisp and pure,
Hearts entwined, we feel secure.
Outside the world, a glistening white,
Inside, we're wrapped in love's delight.

A Symphony of Comfort Amidst the Snow

Snowflakes fall, a gentle tune,
Under stars and the watchful moon.
Each flake carries a fleeting dream,
In the stillness, we find our theme.

Hot chocolate warms our chilled hands,
As we share our whispered plans.
With friends gathered, joy takes flight,
A symphony played on a snowy night.

Serendipity Found in Mugs

Steam rises from the cups we hold,
Stories shared, memories unfold.
Every sip brings us closer still,
Comfort brews in a porcelain thrill.

Cinnamon whispers in the air,
Wrapped in laughter, time goes nowhere.
With every toast, our spirits lift,
In these moments, we find our gift.

The Touch of Magic in a Glass

Each pour is like a spell, you see,
Shimmering whispers of tranquility.
The clink of glasses, spirits soar,
In warmth and cheer, we seek for more.

Gelid nights meet fragrant grace,
Every sip a sweet embrace.
With friends beside, we chase despair,
In the magic found within our glass.

Charmed by the Chill

Whispers of winter dance in the air,
Soft snowflakes twirl without a care.
Frost-kissed trees stand tall and bright,
Nature's canvas, purest white.

Gathered around in cozy nooks,
With warm drinks and well-worn books.
Fireplace crackles, shadows play,
Charmed by the chill, we find our way.

Comforted by the Heat

Sunrise spills gold on warming ground,
Radiant beams, a safe surround.
Ember glow releases the night,
Comforted by the heat, we unite.

With shared laughter, stories soar,
Every moment, we cherish more.
In warmth we find a loving space,
Where all worries slowly erase.

Nurturing Spirits with Every Sip

In every cup, a journey flows,
To distant lands where comfort grows.
Herbs and spices, whispers of days,
Nurturing spirits in countless ways.

Warmth envelops, a gentle embrace,
Filling hearts, a soothing grace.
Savor the moment, let it unfold,
With every sip, a treasure untold.

The Poetry of Steam Against the Cold

Steam rises softly, a whispered rhyme,
A dance of warmth defying time.
Each droplet glistens, a fleeting kiss,
In winter's grasp, we find our bliss.

The kettle sings its sweet refrain,
A melody to soothe the pain.
In steaming cups, solace awaits,
The poetry of steam, love creates.

Embracing Winter's Heart with Gentle Flavors

Cinnamon whispers, a sweet allure,
Nutmeg stirs dreams, warm and pure.
In every bite, winter's embrace,
Gentle flavors, time slows its race.

Wrapped in scarves, we taste the chill,
With every morsel, we find the thrill.
Embracing winter, our spirits lift,
In shared delights, the season's gift.

Enveloping Chills

The cold wind whispers low,
As frosty breath does flow.
Each step upon the ground,
Echoes winter's silent sound.

Beneath the sky so gray,
Footprints slowly fade away.
In layers, warmth we seek,
While nature's heart turns bleak.

Inviting Brews

Steam rises in the air,
A fragrant pot we share.
Cinnamon and spice blend,
As laughter seems to send.

Mugs cradled in our hands,
In warmth, each moment stands.
With every sip, we find,
A comfort intertwined.

Winter Conversations in Warm Hues

In cozy corners, we sit tight,
With stories shared, hearts light.
The fire glows and sparks fly,
As outside, snowflakes sigh.

Laughter dances in the room,
Chasing away the cold gloom.
In hues of amber and gold,
We weave our joy, manifold.

Warm Brews on Frosty Mornings

Morning sun peeks through the frost,
As warmth is never lost.
Coffee brews, filling the air,
With every sip, joy is rare.

Outside, the world is white,
In here, everything feels right.
Wrapped in blankets, we embrace,
The beauty of this place.

Whispering Flakes in the Cozy Air

Softly falling from the sky,
Whispering flurries drift by.
In the stillness, time stands still,
As blankets cover every hill.

Inside, the warmth ignites,
In candle's glow, soft lights.
Every flake a tale to tell,
In this winter's magic spell.

Whispers of Joy in Chilly Mornings

Morning light breaks soft and clear,
Whispers of joy linger near.
Frosted leaves dance in the breeze,
Nature's palette, colors please.

Birds chirp sweetly, hearts take flight,
In the glow of morning light.
Every breath, a frosty puff,
In this moment, life feels enough.

Laughter echoes in the air,
Chilly fingers, souls laid bare.
The world awakens, fresh and bright,
Whispers of joy in pure delight.

The Embrace of Heat in Frosty Hands

Frosty hands reach for the fire,
Embers glow with warm desire.
Cocoas swirl in mugs held tight,
Each sip brings comfort, pure delight.

Outside, the world's a snowy sea,
But here we choose to simply be.
Wrapped in warmth, our hearts ignite,
In the embrace of heat, all feels right.

Laughter dances, shadows play,
With every moment, we delay.
As winter whispers through the night,
The glow of warmth sustains our light.

Capturing Winter in a Warm Brew

Snowflakes fall, a gentle hush,
In a moment, winter's crush.
Cup in hand, I take a sip,
Warmth surrounds, my soul does flip.

Steaming aromas fill the air,
Cinnamon, chocolate everywhere.
Each taste a journey, rich and bold,
Capturing winter, stories told.

Sipping slowly by the glow,
In this cocoon, time moves slow.
With every swirl, a memory stirs,
Wrapped in warmth, the heart concurs.

Sweet Brews in a Winter's Tale

Winter nights hold magic's sway,
Sweet brews guide the heart's ballet.
Lemon, honey, ginger zest,
In every cup, the soul finds rest.

Whispers of spice, a fragrant spell,
Stories woven, hearts compel.
With friends around, the laughter flows,
In every sip, the warmth bestows.

Candles flicker, shadows dance,
In this moment, we take a chance.
To share the warmth, the joy, the light,
In winter's tale, everything feels right.

Snowflakes Dance on the Glistening Window

Snowflakes twirl in the soft, cold air,
Drifting softly without a care.
They land gently, covering all,
A white blanket, the world's soft call.

The window fogs with breath so warm,
Creating a cozy, inviting charm.
Patterns weave in icy lace,
As winter whispers in its embrace.

Outside, the world is hushed and still,
Snowflakes dance, a magical thrill.
In silence, they fall, a soft parade,
Painting the night with a shimmering shade.

Each flake unique, a story untold,
In the arms of winter, we feel the cold.
Together they fall, a beautiful sight,
Snowflakes dance softly, filling the night.

A Mug of Joy in the Flurry

In the kitchen, warmth abounds,
A gentle hum of happy sounds.
Steam rises from a mug held tight,
A moment cherished on a winter's night.

Cocoa swirls, rich and divine,
Marshmallows float, sweet and fine.
With each sip, the world slows down,
Joy fills the heart, erasing the frown.

The storm outside begins to roar,
Yet here inside, there's so much more.
Laughter dances, fires crackle bright,
Together we savor this pure delight.

A mug of joy in winter's embrace,
As flurries swirl beyond our space.
In fleeting moments, love does bloom,
A serenity found in this cozy room.

Frost-Kissed Whispers of Enchantment

Frost-kissed branches gently sway,
Under moonlight, they softly play.
The chill of night holds secrets deep,
Enchanting dreams in silence seep.

Whispers carry through the trees,
A lullaby borne on the breeze.
Each breath of winter, crisp and bright,
Holds magic woven in the night.

Footsteps crunch on fresh, white snow,
As shadows dance in the mellow glow.
Frosted air, a calming balm,
Crafting moments softly calm.

Nature holds its breath in peace,
A tranquil spell that will not cease.
In this splendor, hearts shall soar,
Frost-kissed whispers forevermore.

Tranquil Moments on a Chilly Evening

The world outside is wrapped in white,
A peaceful hush, the day's twilight.
Candles flicker, shadows play,
Tranquil moments at the end of the day.

Warmth radiates from the fire's light,
As we gather, hearts feel right.
Wrapped in blankets, we sit as one,
Chasing away the chill till it's gone.

Sipping tea, the flavors blend,
Every note a gentle friend.
Stories shared, laughter flies,
In this warmth, no one sighs.

As stars twinkle in the vast, dark dome,
In this quiet, we find our home.
Chilly evenings draw us near,
In tranquil moments, love holds dear.

A Cozy Embrace of Flavor and Frost

In the hearth's soft glow, we find our grace,
Spices twirl and dance, in a warm embrace.
A cup in hand, with laughter we share,
Flavors mingle sweetly, free from all care.

Snowflakes fall, the world turns bright,
Wrapped in blankets, we hold on tight.
Sip by sip, the warmth flows through,
In this cozy haven, love feels anew.

Frost's Gentle Touch on Warm Brews

Morning light spills on frosted panes,
A gentle whisper, the winter remains.
Steaming mugs clutched, hands come alive,
In this moment, our spirits thrive.

The crisp air nips, yet we feel so bold,
Stories unfold, as the day takes hold.
Frost outside, but inside it's bright,
With every sip, we chase away night.

Whispers of Warmth in the Winter's Grip

In the chill of dusk, fires crackle low,
The scent of pine, and embers aglow.
With whispers soft, our worries fade,
In this winter's story, joy is made.

A quilt of warmth, wrapped around our dreams,
Hot cider and laughter, flowing like streams.
Through the frosty veil, we find our way,
Together in warmth, we'll greet the day.

Quiet Comforts Amidst the Ice

Silence blankets the world in white,
Nestled in comfort, the stars shine bright.
Softly we breathe, in the stillness we know,
That warmth in our hearts makes the cold ebb and flow.

The kettle sings sweet, as night drapes its shawl,
In gentle embrace, we let warmth befall.
Through the icy panes, love softly flows,
In quiet moments, our true heat grows.

Toasty Hues Beneath a White Blanket

Fires crackle, warm and bright,
Surrounded by a cozy light.
Golden amber, deep and bold,
Stories whispered, tales retold.

Outside, snowflakes dance and twirl,
Nature dons her frosty pearl.
Inside, the hearth, a glowing gem,
Comfort lives in each warm hem.

Blankets draped, soft and thick,
Time slows down, our hearts they pick.
Toasty hues in twilight's glow,
Beneath the blanket, love will grow.

Serenity Brought by Hot Elixirs

Steam rises from a mug held tight,
Gentle aroma, pure delight.
Herbal whispers soothe the soul,
Each sip a comfort, making whole.

Calm descends like evening stars,
In the moment, forget the scars.
Warmth envelops, peace unfurls,
Serenity in swirling whirls.

Golden chai or rich cocoa,
Each elixir's a gentle flow.
In this stillness, heartbeats blend,
Hot comforts, our dear friends.

Melodies of Snow and Brew

Soft snowflakes kiss the ground,
In the silence, peace is found.
Coffee brews with fragrant rise,
A melody beneath the skies.

Whispers of winter wrap the day,
Gentle rhythms, warm ballet.
Sips of warmth, a sweet refrain,
In the stillness, joy remains.

Each note of snowflakes, soft and light,
Joined by warmth, a sweet delight.
Brewed creations fill the air,
Melodies of love, we share.

Gentle Sips as Flurries Fall

By the window, watching snow,
Flurries dance, a softening flow.
With each sip, the world grows still,
Gentle warmth brings peaceful thrill.

Mugs embrace our eager hands,
As outside, winter softly stands.
A symphony in frosty air,
Wrapped in warmth, love everywhere.

Sipping slow on life's rich brew,
Every flavor feels so true.
In the flurry, hearts unite,
Moments cherished, pure delight.

Warmth that Lingers Longer

In the hearth's soft glow we find,
A comfort shared, souls intertwined.
With laughter bright and stories told,
Embers dance in shades of gold.

A blanket wrapped, a cozy sigh,
The world outside may howl and cry.
But here, the warmth is ours to keep,
In moments sweet, our hearts leap.

The scent of cocoa fills the air,
As joy unravels every care.
In winter's grasp, we stand as one,
Together basking in the sun.

As twilight fades, the stars ignite,
In this embrace, all feels so right.
Here's to the nights that stay so dear,
Where warmth lingers, year to year.

Life's Sweet Escape from the Cold

A journey's tale, we bravely take,
Through frosty paths and trails that wake.
With every step, the chill retreats,
Replaced by sun, where heart feels beats.

We chase the light, where shadows fade,
In tranquil glades, our fears mislaid.
Like whispers soft, the breezes tease,
Awakening joy with gentle ease.

A warm embrace, the soul's delight,
In colorful blooms that greet the night.
No frost can hold what love has grown,
Together we laugh, never alone.

The frost may bite, but we stand bold,
Life's sweet escape from the cold.
With hands entwined, we bask in grace,
Creating warmth in every place.

Moments Captured in Cups

In tiny cups, our stories blend,
With sips of tea, our hearts transcend.
Each flavor sings of times we share,
Warmth in our hands, love in the air.

From morning light till evening's hue,
We pour our dreams, collect the dew.
In every taste, a memory flows,
As laughter rises, sweetness grows.

The clinking mugs, a joyful sound,
In simple rituals, joy is found.
With every brew, a moment's bliss,
Inviting peace in every kiss.

So raise your cup, let spirits soar,
In line with friends, we ask for more.
These moments cherished, forever up,
Life's essence found in every cup.

Light Flickering in a Snowy Dream

Through frosted panes, the world aglow,
A dance of light on purest snow.
Each flake that falls, a whispered prayer,
In winter's hush, we find our care.

The candle's flame, a soft embrace,
Illuminates each gentle face.
With shadows long and stories spun,
In this serene dance, we become one.

Outside, the chill may seek to bite,
But in our hearts, there burns a light.
With every flicker, dreams take flight,
In snowy realms, we find our sight.

So let it snow, let time suspend,
In this dream, we shall not end.
With light that flickers, warm and bright,
Forever cherished, day and night.

Serene Brews Under Glittering Skies

In gardens where soft whispers sway,
Leaves dance beneath the golden ray.
Breezes carry a soothing tune,
As tea steams gently under the moon.

Stars twinkle in the velvet dark,
The world around me leaves its mark.
With every sip, tranquility flows,
In tranquil spots where silence grows.

A cup cradled in tender hands,
Welcoming calm as the night expands.
Brews of jasmine, sweet and bright,
Bathe the heart in pure delight.

So raise your cup to skies so grand,
For every brew, a dream to stand.
In each sip, a moment here,
Serene and bright, the night is clear.

Heartfelt Brews in a Winter Wonderland

Snowflakes drift on the chilly breeze,
Winter's charm puts the heart at ease.
Cocoa warms my awaiting hands,
In this cozy, enchanting land.

Fire crackles with a gentle glow,
Outside, the world is draped in snow.
With each sip, warmth embraces tight,
In heartfelt brews that feel just right.

Whispers of love in every cup,
Gather around; let the spirits up.
Snow-drenched trees frame the twilight,
As laughter rings through the frosty night.

In this winter, we find our song,
Over brews, we always belong.
Let's treasure moments, brave and bold,
In winter's tale, let love unfold.

A Bow to Fortune in a Cup

In delicate porcelain, luck resides,
Every brew a chance that glides.
Fragrant leaves steeped with care,
Upon each sip, fortune lays bare.

With a sprinkle of sweet, a dash of spice,
In every flavor, life's delight.
Raise your cup to dreams and fate,
For destiny's dance we celebrate.

A sip of hope, a swirl of cheer,
Inviting fortune, drawing it near.
Each taste whispers soft, profound,
In every moment, magic is found.

A bow to the lessons in each brew,
For life's rich tapestry ever anew.
In every cup, a treasure untold,
Where fortune and love entwine so bold.

Snowy Days and Steamy Nights

Snowflakes fall in a soft embrace,
Covering the world with gentle grace.
A steaming cup warms my weary soul,
In this winter haven, I feel whole.

Candles flicker in the dusky light,
As cozy blankets make the scene right.
With every sip, the night unfolds,
Stories exchanged as the warmth holds.

Frosty windows tell tales outside,
While inside, laughter serves as guide.
In frothy mugs of rich delight,
We chase the chill with hearts so bright.

So let the snow dance in the air,
While lovely brews are shared with care.
In snowy days, we find our cheer,
With steamy nights that draw us near.

Steam Rising in the Silent Night

In the stillness, whispers rise,
Steam escaping, touching skies.
Moonlit shadows dance and sway,
Night enfolds the close of day.

Muffled echoes, soft and deep,
Secrets that the night can keep.
Sipping warmth beneath the glow,
Tender moments, silent flow.

Frost clings lightly to the pane,
A world asleep, yet not in vain.
Each breath captured, soft and sweet,
In the quiet, hearts can meet.

With every drop, the warmth ignites,
Uniting spirits in the nights.
Steam rising, dreams take flight,
In this moment, all feels right.

Caffeine Dreams Under a Snowy Veil

Snowflakes dance like whispered sighs,
Caffeine warmth beneath cold skies.
In a cup, a world unfolds,
Stories brewed in rich brown gold.

Chasing dreams on winds so free,
Underneath this snowy spree.
Each sip ignites a spark of cheer,
Binding moments, drawing near.

Fleeting thoughts like snowflakes fall,
In the haze, I hear the call.
Caffeine dreams swirl in the air,
Wrapped in warmth, a tender care.

Steaming mugs in winter's grasp,
Hearts entwined with every clasp.
In the chill, we find our grace,
Caffeine dreams, a warm embrace.

The Aroma of Winter's Heart

A fragrant kiss from winter's breath,
In the air, a dance with death.
Spices swirl, the world enthralls,
Embracing warmth as winter calls.

The aroma stirs within my soul,
A comforting, familiar role.
Each note a memory wrapped in time,
Infusing life with every rhyme.

Cinnamon, cloves, and cocoa sweet,
Drawing forth the joy we need.
In this season, clear and bright,
We find our way, igniting light.

Through the frosty window's view,
The world awaits, refreshed and new.
Aroma of winter, bold and clear,
Filling hearts with love and cheer.

Refuge in a Delicate Sip

In a cup, find calm and peace,
A gentle sip, sweet release.
Warmth envelops, soft and light,
In this refuge, all feels right.

Leaves of tea dance as they steep,
Awakening dreams from their sleep.
Moments freeze, the world outside,
In this warmth, I'll always hide.

Delicate notes of jasmine bloom,
Filling up the quiet room.
With every breath, the worries fade,
Peace is found, and fears are laid.

Sipping slowly, savoring each,
In this place, no lessons to teach.
A refuge from the stormy tide,
In a delicate sip, I abide.

The Harmony of Taste in Winter Stillness

In stillness deep, where whispers glide,
Flavors blend, like snowflakes wide.
Warm spices dance in evening's chill,
A symphony of taste, a winter thrill.

Lemon zest and cinnamon twine,
In mugs of cheer, our hearts align.
Each sip brings tales of fireside glow,
As frost unfolds in a gentle flow.

Beneath a quilt of silver light,
We savor warmth in the calm of night.
Nuts and berries, a sweet embrace,
Nature's bounty, a cozy space.

In harmony, our senses meet,
With every taste, the season's heat.
Together, in this frosty bliss,
The winter's magic, we will not miss.

Snowy Adventures with a Warm Sip

Snowflakes whirl, the world is bright,
Adventure calls in the soft moonlight.
With steaming mugs, we venture free,
In crisp white trails, just you and me.

Sledding down hills with laughter loud,
A cup of cocoa, under the cloud.
Marshmallows float, sweet dreams in sight,
Our hearts aglow, in winter's light.

Frozen branches shimmer like gold,
Stories shared, as the night unfolds.
Exhilaration in each frosty breath,
Moments cherished, defying death.

With every sip, memories blend,
In snowy adventures, love we tend.
Together we journey, hand in hand,
In warmth and joy, forever we stand.

Welcoming Winter with a Toast

As winter whispers with gentle breath,
We raise our glasses, a toast to zest.
Crisp apple cider, spiced just right,
In the chilly air, we find delight.

Friends gather round the warming fire,
With hearty laughter, our spirits aspire.
Roasted nuts and seasonal cheer,
Each sip brings warmth when loved ones near.

Frosty windows, a sparkling view,
We share our wishes, old and new.
Candles flicker in a cozy glow,
In every toast, our fondness grows.

Together we welcome this snowy reign,
With hearts entwined, like soft, sweet rain.
In winter's embrace, we find our place,
Warmth in toasting, a sacred space.

The Joy of Savoring Frosty Moments

The whispering wind, a frosty morn,
In every breath, winter is born.
Sipping tea as snowflakes play,
Each moment cherished, come what may.

Furry blankets wrap us tight,
While outside dances the chilly night.
Ginger cookies, warm from the bake,
Smiles abound, as hearts awake.

Nature's art on every pane,
Frosty patterns, a sweet refrain.
We gather close, with stories told,
In winter's joy, our spirits bold.

The magic lingers in every taste,
These frosty moments, we'll not waste.
Winter's embrace, so rich and bright,
A treasure shared, in soft twilight.

Moments of Bliss in the Snowy Silence

In winter's hush, the world stands still,
Soft flakes drift down, a gentle thrill.
Branches cradle the white embrace,
Embracing peace, in a quiet space.

Footsteps faint, the ground adorned,
Whispers of nature, a beauty born.
Every breath, a frosty sigh,
In this moment, we feel the sky.

Children laugh, their spirits soar,
The joy they find, we all adore.
Snowmen rise with buttoned eyes,
In snowy silence, our hearts reply.

The evening glows, silence sings,
Wrapped in warmth, the magic clings.
Each moment pure, like freshly fallen snow,
In blissful silence, together we grow.

Infusions of Warmth in a Frozen Realm

Frosted windows, a view so bright,
Inside the glow, we hold on tight.
Teas and spices, the kettle sings,
Sipping warmth as winter clings.

The dance of flames, the crackling cheer,
Stories shared, loved ones near.
Cinnamon swirls, and cocoa's delight,
Each infusion, pure winter's bite.

With every sip, the chill retreats,
A cozy blanket, tender seats.
Frozen landscapes, a wonderland,
Inside, we weave our dreams unplanned.

As snowflakes glide, we taste the night,
In this realm, our hearts take flight.
Infusions warm, both rich and sweet,
In frozen beauty, our souls meet.

Hot Brews and Winter Whispers

A kettle whistles, a song so sweet,
Steaming bubbles in rhythmic beat.
Spiced chai dances in porcelain grace,
Whispers of warmth in a chilly place.

Outside, the world, a canvas white,
Inside, our hearts radiate light.
With each hot brew, the candle glows,
Winter whispers as the cold wind blows.

Sip by sip, we gather near,
In fragrant trails, we conquer fear.
Every sip, a memory made,
In this haven, our worries fade.

Laughter mingles with the steam,
Creating moments, a waking dream.
Hot brews shared, in quiet night,
In winter's arms, we feel so right.

Solace in a Cup

A simple cup, a world contained,
In steamy swirls, our hearts unchained.
Every sip, a soothing balm,
In winter's chill, we find our calm.

Fingers wrapped 'round warmth divine,
Moments pause, as stars align.
Cocoa richness, honey's sweet,
In this solace, our souls meet.

Silence speaks, the clock stands still,
In fragrant dreams, we find our will.
This sacred hour, a cherished space,
In every cup, we leave a trace.

Toasting life with each warm cheer,
In every sip, love reappears.
Solace found, as fires burn,
In winter's grasp, it's our turn.

Enveloped in Cozy Fragrance

The scent of pine drifts through the air,
With candles flickering, casting cheer.
A warm embrace, a soft, sweet flair,
Moments cherished, held near and dear.

Laughter dances like a gentle breeze,
Wrapped in blankets, we softly lay.
Cup of cocoa, delight that frees,
Time slows down, all worries sway.

Whispers of love in every scent,
A heart full of warmth, souls entwined.
Memories crafted, so splendidly meant,
In this haven, true joy we find.

The world outside grows dim and cold,
But inside glows a radiant light.
In this fragrance, stories unfold,
A tapestry woven, pure and bright.

Heartwarming Flavors Amidst the Frost

Chilled air biting, but hearts beat warm,
Spices mingle, wrapped with care.
A feast awaits, safe from the storm,
Family gathered, love in the air.

Pumpkin pie with whipped cream swirls,
Cinnamon rolls fresh from the oven.
Each taste a memory, heart unfurls,
In every bite, affection's woven.

Steamy soup in bowls, hands around,
Laughter spills like warmth from the stove.
In these flavors, solace is found,
Hearts share stories, together we rove.

As frost paints windows, love is alive,
In the kitchen, bonds intertwine.
With every flavor, our spirits thrive,
In this moment, everything's divine.

Reflections of Joy in a Chilly Room

Windows frosted with winter's breath,
Inside, warmth radiates and glows.
Flickering lights break the cold's depth,
Every corner with comfort flows.

A soft blanket wrapped around tight,
Glimmers of joy dance in our eyes.
Sharing moments from day to night,
Wrapped in laughter, love never dies.

Old stories shared with warmth anew,
Memories dance like shadows on wall.
The chill outside, we bid adieu,
In our hearts, laughter's the call.

Reflections of joy in every glance,
In a chilly room, we come alive.
With every heartbeat, a sweet romance,
Together we flourish, together we thrive.

Gentle Embrace of Fire and Ice

Snowflakes twirl in a ballet of grace,
While shadows flicker from the hearth.
A dance of warmth meets winter's face,
Beauty rests in this mirthful earth.

Crackling flames whisper tales untold,
As icy breath kisses the pane.
The heart finds solace, a stronghold,
In this embrace where peace can reign.

Glowing embers like stars in the night,
Frosty patterns paint the world outside.
In this moment, a bond feels right,
Where fire and ice harmoniously hide.

With a gentle sway, we find our place,
Amidst the duality of night and day.
Together we journey, hearts interlace,
In the gentle embrace, come what may.

Whispers in the Winter Breeze

Silent glimmers in the night,
Shadows dance in pale moonlight.
Frosty whispers paint the trees,
As the world sways with the breeze.

Frozen breath in crisp, still air,
Winter's touch is everywhere.
Softly falling, snowflakes glow,
Nature's hush, a silent show.

Footprints crunch on frosted ground,
Echoes of a world profound.
Wrapped in warmth, the night enfolds,
Whispers of a tale retold.

In the quiet, secrets lay,
Winter's charm will softly sway.
As stars twinkle through the chill,
Time stands still, the heart does fill.

Brews Beneath a Blanketed Sky

Steam arises in the glow,
Cups of warmth in hand we know.
Beneath blankets of cosmic light,
Sipping dreams, hearts take flight.

Warmth cascades in gentle streams,
Brews that spark the brightest dreams.
In the night, our stories flow,
Fingers wrapped in joy's soft glow.

Amidst the stars, a world divine,
The sky weaves tales, both yours and mine.
With each sip, a spark ignites,
Creating joy on chilly nights.

Together, we embrace the dark,
In each other, we find our spark.
Brews shared beneath the sky so wide,
In the hush of night, dreams collide.

Ember Warmth on Frosty Mornings

Morning light through window gleams,
Embers crackle, waking dreams.
Frosty glass and breath like smoke,
In this haven, hearts invoke.

Sipping slowly, time suspends,
Wrapped in warmth, the spirit mends.
Muffled sounds of life appear,
As cozy whispers draw us near.

Outside, winter's chill may bite,
Yet inside glows a steady light.
Each moment, tender and clear,
Ember warmth, forever dear.

In the quiet, peace will flow,
Through our hearts, the fire glows.
Frosted mornings softly sing,
In their arms, new warmth they bring.

Sips of Solitude in Silvery Silence

In the dusk, the world stands still,
Sips of solitude, a gentle thrill.
Lunar glow in quiet grace,
Silvery silence, a warm embrace.

Each drop a moment, pure and bright,
Lost reflections in the night.
Thoughts drift like clouds on the breeze,
In this peace, my heart finds ease.

Whispers linger, soft and low,
The night reveals what few may know.
Under stars, I find my way,
Sips of solitude, night to day.

Time slows down, and dreams ignite,
In solitude, I find the light.
With every sip, the silence sings,
A symphony that solitude brings.

Sips of Comfort Amidst the Chill

A steaming cup warms my hands,
As winter winds brush against the strands.
Each sip a whisper, soft and kind,
In every drop, solace I find.

Frosty breaths dance in the air,
While candlelight flickers, bright and fair.
With every moment, worries cease,
Sips of comfort, bringing peace.

The world outside, a glistening white,
Yet here, it feels just right tonight.
Embraced by warmth, I softly sigh,
In this small haven, spirits fly.

As snowflakes twirl and gently fall,
I hold my love close, feeling small.
In this winter's heart we'll remain,
Sips of joy, a sweet refrain.

Constellations of Frosted Glass

Outside the window, stars unfold,
In icy patterns, tales retold.
Each breath a puff, a secret shared,
In frosted glass, dreams are snared.

The night sky twinkles, pure and bright,
As shadows dance in soft moonlight.
Each flake a gem, the world aglow,
In silvery trails, our whispers flow.

Gathered softly by the fire's glow,
Where memories and laughter flow.
In this winter's deep embrace,
Constellations twine, time and space.

These tiny worlds, a frozen art,
Mirror our hopes, reflect the heart.
Life's gentle warmth we hold so dear,
In constellations, winter's cheer.

Solace in a Winter Embrace

Blanketed skies in shades of gray,
Yet warmth resides where hearts hold sway.
In the hush of snow, a peace descends,
Solace found in winter's bends.

Cocoa swirls with marshmallow dreams,
A melody sweet, like soft moonbeams.
Wrapped in layers, feelings ignite,
In winter's embrace, everything feels right.

Footprints mark tales in the snow,
As laughter erupts from deep below.
Every moment, a dance with the cold,
Together we weave, our stories told.

Under the stars, with hearts aligned,
In winter's arms, love is defined.
With whispered vows, we find our place,
In this season, pure and embraced.

Liquid Warmth Against the White

In a cup of dreams, warmth resides,
Flowing gently, as the chill subsides.
Golden fluid, rich and sweet,
A remedy found, a simple treat.

Outside, the world dons a frosty cloak,
While inside, we laugh and softly joke.
Each sip a hug, a gentle sigh,
Liquid warmth, as snowflakes fly.

With friends and family gathered near,
Every smile brings the heart cheer.
In every drop, memories blend,
Against the white, love transcends.

As the evening drifts into the night,
We toast with cups, all feels right.
In winter's grasp, our spirits glow,
Liquid warmth, as soft winds blow.

Chasing Clouds with Warmth in Hand

In the sky, dreams drift and sway,
Floating softly through the day.
With hands wrapped tight around a cup,
We chase the clouds, never giving up.

Sunlit paths beneath our feet,
Life's a dance, a wondrous beat.
Warmth is found in every sip,
As laughter bubbles, hearts do skip.

Through fields of gold, we wander free,
Chasing shadows, just you and me.
With every breeze, our spirits soar,
Together, love, we'll always explore.

In the twilight, colors blend,
Moments like these, they never end.
With warmth in hand, we'll roam forever,
Chasing clouds, our hearts tethered.

Cocoa Dreams in Icy Realms

In the still of winter's night,
Cocoa dreams take gentle flight.
Marshmallows dance in steaming streams,
Whisking us away to sweet themes.

Under blankets, spirits rise,
Glistening stars in velvet skies.
Sipping slowly, we embrace,
Magic woven, time can't erase.

Icy realms outside our door,
Yet in our hearts, warmth does pour.
With every taste, a world unfolds,
Cocoa dreams, a treasure to hold.

As snowflakes fall and silence reigns,
Love's sweet echo gently remains.
In the glow of the fire's light,
Cocoa dreams keep us warm tonight.

Mugs of Comfort Amidst the Chill

Mugs of comfort, hands held tight,
In the chill of the crisp moonlight.
With every sip, the ice will fade,
Creating warmth in luscious shades.

A crackling fire, shadows dance,
Moments cherished, the perfect chance.
Here we gather, laughter shared,
In cozy corners, hearts declared.

Gazing out at winter's grace,
We find our joy in this warm space.
Steam spirals up, a gentle sight,
Together here, everything feels right.

Mugs of comfort held so dear,
Chasing away the frost and fear.
With every chuckle, warmth ignites,
This simple pleasure, pure delights.

Frosty Windows, Cozy Moments

Frosty windows, patterns bright,
Nature's art in morning light.
Inside, the world feels so serene,
Cozy moments, where we convene.

With whispers soft, we share our dreams,
In hot cocoa with whipped cream.
The chill outside, a distant hum,
In this haven, our hearts succumb.

Laughter spills like melting snow,
In these moments, love will grow.
With every breath, warmth fills the air,
Cozy moments, none can compare.

Frosty windows reflect our glee,
Together wrapped in harmony.
Life unfolds in delight's embrace,
In our little, cherished space.

The Dance of Vapors and White Flurries

In the quiet air, vapors twirl,
Whispers of warmth in a winter whirl.
Flurries float down, soft and light,
A dance of white in the fading light.

Clouds cascade, a shroud of gray,
Together they drift, then softly sway.
Each breath we take, a misty plume,
Painting the world with winter's bloom.

Savoring Heat on a Snowy Day

As snowflakes flutter, we huddle near,
Inside, where the warmth feels ever dear.
Steam rises gently from mugs of cheer,
Savoring every sip, winter's premier.

The world outside, a blanket of white,
While inside glows with a soft, golden light.
We share our stories, laughter, and dreams,
Embracing the chill, in cozy extremes.

Liquid Warmth Against a Winter Canvas

A canvas of frost, white and bright,
We cradle warmth in the chilly night.
Tea leaves infuse a fragrant embrace,
Liquid warmth blooms in every space.

The snow paints paths as we stroll outside,
With every sip, the cold we bide.
Together we linger, hearts intertwined,
In winter's embrace, our souls aligned.

Flakes and Brews: A Seasonal Harmony

Falling gently, the snowflakes land,
While in our cups, warm dreams expand.
Brews of spice, rich and deep,
A melody of flavors, sweet to keep.

Outside the world, a frosty show,
But inside, we bask in the cozy glow.
Flakes and brews create their song,
A seasonal harmony, where we belong.

Radiance Within the Frozen Realm

In the quiet of the snow,
A light begins to glow.
Whispers of warmth arise,
Underneath the frozen skies.

Icicles glint in the sun,
Reflecting joy, a spark begun.
Through frosted branches, bright and clear,
Nature's beauty, drawing near.

In this realm of white and blue,
Hope emerges, fresh and new.
Every shadow finds its light,
In the winter, pure delight.

Embracing all the silent charms,
Winter's grip, with all its arms.
Radiance shines within the cold,
A story of warmth, silently told.

Cozy Moments Wrapped in Flakes

Snowflakes dance upon the ground,
Each unique, a sight profound.
Hot cocoa warms our hands,
As winter's magic brightly stands.

Fires crackle, shadows play,
In cozy corners, we will stay.
Blankets wrapped around so tight,
In these moments, hearts feel right.

Laughter echoes, stories shared,
With loved ones, we are spared.
Whispers soft as moonlit dreams,
Together warm, or so it seems.

Every flake a gentle sigh,
Falling softly from the sky.
In joy, we find our perfect place,
Cozy moments, wrapped in grace.

Pouring Happiness in Cold Light

With every snowflake that descends,
A promise of joy that never ends.
Frosty breath and cheerful glow,
In the cold, our spirits grow.

Laughter spills like melting snow,
Warming hearts, a gentle flow.
Hot drinks shared by fire's glow,
Together where the love can show.

Wind whispers tales of the past,
Moments we cherish, joys amassed.
As magic dances in the night,
We pour happiness into the light.

Under stars, our dreams take flight,
Wrapped in blankets, holding tight.
In these chilly nights, we find,
The warmth within, forever kind.

The Beauty of Warmth in Winter's Grasp

In winter's grasp, we find our peace,
A world transformed, a sweet release.
Snowflakes twirl like soft ballet,
While fires crackle, chase gloom away.

Golden rays through frosty air,
Painting landscapes, pure and rare.
The beauty glows in every hue,
Nature's canvas, fresh and new.

Moments spent, hand in hand,
Together we make every strand.
With love aglow in bitter cold,
Our hearts embrace the stories told.

Warmed by friendship, laughter's spark,
Together lighting up the dark.
In winter's hold, we truly see,
The beauty of warmth, you and me.

Snow-Dusted Dreams in a Thermal Embrace

In the quiet night of winter's glow,
Snowflakes whisper secrets below.
Wrapped in blankets, we find our peace,
As dreams of warmth and love increase.

Crisp air bites, but hearts are warm,
Inside these walls, away from harm.
Fires crackle, casting shadows high,
While snowflakes dance like stars in the sky.

Hands entwined, we share our hopes,
In this embrace, together we cope.
Every flake a story, a silent song,
In our little world, we both belong.

Beneath the moon's soft, glowing light,
We seal our dreams with stars so bright.
Snow-dusted moments, tender and true,
In thermal warmth, I find you.

The Comfort of Chocolate and Chill

A chilly breeze, the fire's glow,
Hot cocoa bubbles, inviting slow.
Marshmallows dance on frothy waves,
In this moment, my spirit saves.

Chocolate whispers sweet and deep,
As winter's secrets softly creep.
Each sip a hug, warm and tight,
Turning cold into pure delight.

Wrapped in layers, outside it's bleak,
Yet in this warmth, we hardly speak.
The comfort found in cocoa's grace,
A tender smile, the heart's embrace.

Through windows fogged with nature's breath,
We sip and share, defying death.
With every taste, our worries fade,
In the simple joy that we've made.

Embracing Winter's Gentle Touch

Winter whispers, soft and slow,
Blankets of white, a serene glow.
Trees stand tall, all draped in lace,
Nature's beauty, a timeless grace.

Frosty breath in the morning light,
Each step crunches, a pure delight.
Silence reigns in this snowy land,
While winter cradles us in its hand.

Winds may howl, but hearts engage,
In this season, we turn the page.
A cozy fire, laughter and cheer,
Embracing winter, we draw near.

The world transforms, all cold and bright,
In its embrace, everything feels right.
Each snowflake a gift from the sky,
Together we'll laugh, together we'll sigh.

Warmth Cradled in Porcelain Hands

Porcelain cup, a delicate hold,
Warmth inside, against the cold.
Steam rises softly, kisses the air,
In small moments, love we share.

The world outside may chill and freeze,
But here we are, wrapped in ease.
With every sip, memories flow,
In porcelain hands, our hearts aglow.

Fingers trace the rim so fine,
A quiet moment, yours and mine.
The comfort found in simple things,
A warm embrace that winter brings.

In flickering lights, the shadows dance,
With porcelain cups, we take a chance.
This warmth we cradled, a perfect blend,
In every sip, love knows no end.

A Dance of Warmth and Frost

In the chill of a winter's night,
Snowflakes gather, pure and white.
Hearts beat warm, a gentle glow,
As laughter dances through the snow.

Frosty air, a breath so clear,
Winter's chill brings friends near.
In the glow of candlelight,
We share our warmth, a sweet delight.

Outside, the world is crisp and bright,
Inside, we hold each other tight.
Nature's rhythm, a soft embrace,
In this moment, we find our place.

As stars twinkle in the dark,
A fire's flicker leaves its mark.
With every sip, we toast the night,
In this dance of warmth and light.

Tasting the Silence of Winter

Snow blankets all with quiet grace,
Each flake a whisper in its place.
The world slows down, the air is still,
In winter's arms, we find our thrill.

Trees stand tall, adorned in white,
A canvas pure, a wondrous sight.
Soft footsteps echo on the lane,
A moment frozen, deep refrain.

With every breath, the frost does bite,
Yet every heart feels warm and light.
We savor silence, crisp and clear,
In winter's hush, we hold it dear.

Each spark of cold, a tale is spun,
In stillness, life has just begun.
Tasting the silence, sweet and bright,
In winter's grip, we find our light.

The Joy in Each Warm Sip

A steaming cup cradled in hand,
Rich flavors swirl, a taste so grand.
With each warm sip, a smile ignites,
Comfort flows through the chilly nights.

Chocolate, spice, or herbal blend,
Each drink a story, a cozy friend.
Steam rises like whispers of cheer,
Inviting moments we hold dear.

By the fire, we gather close,
Tales unfold, laughter engrossed.
In the heart of winter's chill,
Warm sips bring a joyous thrill.

So let us raise our mugs up high,
To warmth that lingers, never shy.
In every drop, love's essence keeps,
The joy in each warm sip, it seeps.

Winter's Whisper in a Mug

A quiet kiss from winter's hand,
In a mug, a warming brand.
With every swirl, it softly sings,
Of cozy nights and gentle things.

Chocolate waves and spices blend,
Each sip a hug, a faithful friend.
Sipping slow, we close our eyes,
In this moment, the world complies.

Snowflakes dance outside the glass,
While in our hearts, warmth will amass.
A whisper of joy, a memory found,
In each small sip, love's spell is bound.

So fill your mug, let worries cease,
In winter's grip, we find our peace.
With every warmth, we come alive,
In winter's whisper, we truly thrive.

Milton Keynes UK
Ingram Content Group UK Ltd.
UKHW021242191124
451300UK00007B/188

9 789916 944622